Welcome to your

SONIC SANCTUARY

A Songweaver's Compendium

TO CREATE YOUR OWN LYRIC LIBRARY

Music is just organized sound: Twelve little tones with their own choreography. But lyrics are infinite. When you combine the lyrics with the music, THAT is how magic is created. I hope that you fill this journal with the thoughts that are in your heart and send those creations out into the world so that more people can heal together through your voice. It matters immensely. Happy creating!

With gratitude and reverence,

Copyright Cadence

www.inomniaparatuspublishing.com

If Music be the
Food of Love?
Play on!

-William
Shakespeare

IDEA GARDEN

Place your imagery, song seeds, and wildcard ideas below!

SONG TITLE

Writers_____ Date:__/__/____

Where Words Fail, Music Speaks

—Hans Christian Andersen

IDEA GARDEN

Place your imagery, song seeds, and wildcard ideas below!

SONG TITLE

Writers_____ Date:__/__/____

Music was my refuge. I could crawl into the space between the notes and curl my back to loneliness

-Maya Angelou

IDEA GARDEN

Place your imagery, song seeds, and wildcard ideas below!

SONG TITLE

Writers_____ Date:__/__/____

Music is the Universal Language of Mankind

-Henry Wadsworth Longfellow

IDEA GARDEN

Place your imagery, song seeds, and wildcard ideas below!

SONG TITLE

Writers_____ Date:__/__/____

Musicians Don't Retire; They stop when there's no more music in them

- Louis Armstrong

IDEA GARDEN

Place your imagery, song seeds, and wildcard ideas below!

SONG TITLE

Writers_____ Date:__/__/____

You know what music is? God's little reminder that there's something else besides us in the Universe: Harmonic Connection between all living beings everywhere. Even the stars

-Robin Williams

IDEA GARDEN

Place your imagery, song seeds, and wildcard ideas below!

SONG TITLE

Writers_____ Date:__/__/____

Music washes away from the soul the dust of everyday life

— Berthold Auerbach

IDEA GARDEN

Place your imagery, song seeds, and wildcard ideas below!

SONG TITLE

Writers_____ Date:__/__/____

That's what music is: entertainment. The more you put yourself into it, the more of you comes out in it.

-Kurt Cobain

IDEA GARDEN

Place your imagery, song seeds, and wildcard ideas below!

SONG TITLE

Writers_____ Date:__/__/____

Music is the Poetry of the Air

-Jean Paul Richter

IDEA GARDEN

Place your imagery, song seeds, and wildcard ideas below!

SONG TITLE

Writers_____ Date:__/__/____

What Passion Cannot Music both Raise & Quell?

- John Dryden

IDEA GARDEN

Place your imagery, song seeds, and wildcard ideas below!

SONG TITLE

Writers_____ Date:__/__/____

Music produces a kind of pleasure which human nature cannot do without

- Confucius

IDEA GARDEN

Place your imagery, song seeds, and wildcard ideas below!

SONG TITLE

Writers_____ Date:__/__/____

Music can change the world because it can change people

-Bono

IDEA GARDEN

Place your imagery, song seeds, and wildcard ideas below!

SONG TITLE

Writers_____ Date:__/__/____

So long as the human spirit thrives on this planet, music in some living form will accompany and sustain it

- Aaron Copland

IDEA GARDEN

Place your imagery, song seeds, and wildcard ideas below!

SONG TITLE

Writers_____ Date:__/__/____

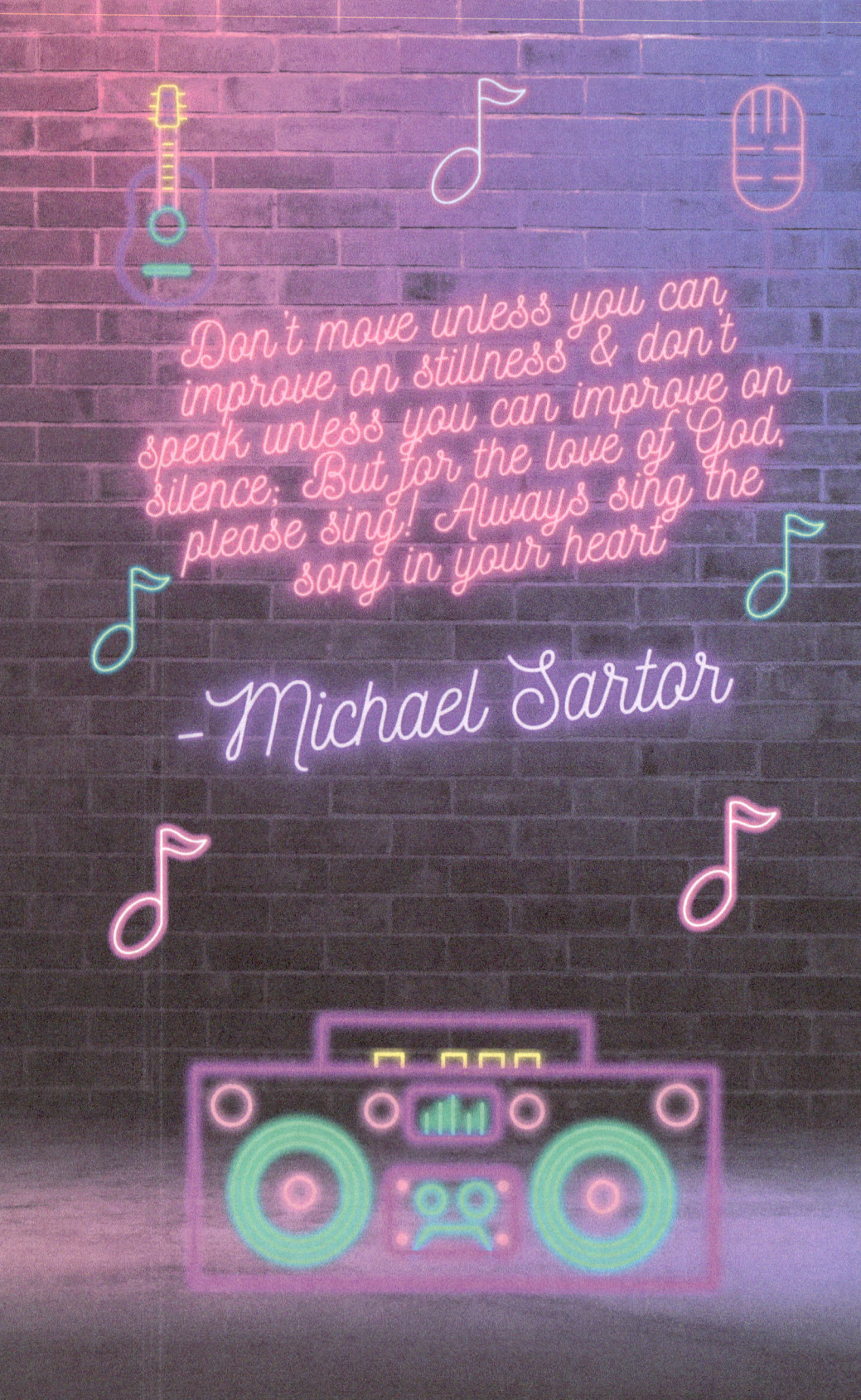

Don't move unless you can improve on stillness & don't speak unless you can improve on silence. But for the love of God, please sing! Always sing the song in your heart

-Michael Sartor

IDEA GARDEN

Place your imagery, song seeds, and wildcard ideas below!

SONG TITLE

Writers_____ Date:__/__/____

I wish you music to help with the burdens of life, and to help you release your happiness to others

- Ludwig Van Beethoven

IDEA GARDEN

Place your imagery, song seeds, and wildcard ideas below!

SONG TITLE

Writers_____ Date:__/__/____

Music fights against the system that teaches to live and die

— Bob Marley

IDEA GARDEN

Place your imagery, song seeds, and wildcard ideas below!

SONG TITLE

Writers_____ Date:__/__/____

When you're happy, you enjoy the music, but when you're sad, you understand the lyrics

-Frank Ocean

IDEA GARDEN

Place your imagery, song seeds, and wildcard ideas below!

SONG TITLE

Writers_____ Date:__/__/____

The beautiful thing is: music can be like a time machine. One song – the lyrics, the melody, the mood – it can take you back to a moment in time like nothing else can

– Lisa Schroeder

IDEA GARDEN

Place your imagery, song seeds, and wildcard ideas below!

SONG TITLE

Writers_____ Date:__/__/____

We think we understand a song's lyrics, but what makes us believe in them, or not - is the music

- Carlos Ruiz Zafron

IDEA GARDEN

Place your imagery, song seeds, and wildcard ideas below!

SONG TITLE

Writers_____ Date:__/__/____

Songwriters write songs, but they really belong to the listener.

-Jimmy Buffet

IDEA GARDEN

Place your imagery, song seeds, and wildcard ideas below!

SONG TITLE

Writers_____ Date:__/__/____

Acknowledgements

THANK YOU ALL

From the Bottom of my Heart

FOR YOUR SUPPORT, LOVE, & BELIEF IN ME & MY CRAZY DREAMS

To my family: especially my parents, my brothers and their partners, all my aunts + uncles, cousins, nieces, nephews and my precious chosen family (you all know who you are.) Thank you doesn't always feel adequate. But thank you just the same.

To my guardian angels Michael Sartor and my grandma Ruby whose presence will never cease to inspire me in this life and the next. Thank you for your passion, and for challenging me to always reach for more. Xo

To Megs and Elysia without whom this journal would never exist. Your kindness, prowess, and compassion means the Universe to me.

And lastly, to all the songweavers out there who have this journal in their hands. I can't wait to hear what you create!

With gratitude and reverence,

Mallory